Betty Gets Ready... For School

Written and Illustrated by

Kathi Greene

AuthorHouse™
1663 Liberty Drive
Bloomington, IN 47403
www.authorhouse.com
Phone: 1 (833) 262-8899

Because of the dynamic nature of the Internet, any web addresses or links contained in this book may have changed
since publication and may no longer be valid. The views expressed in this work are solely those of the author and do
not necessarily reflect the views of the publisher, and the publisher hereby disclaims any responsibility for them.

Any people depicted in stock imagery provided by Getty Images are models,
and such images are being used for illustrative purposes only.
Certain stock imagery © Getty Images.

This book is printed on acid-free paper.

ISBN: 978-1-4259-5888-6 (sc)

Library of Congress Control Number: 2006909592

Print information available on the last page.

Published by AuthorHouse 09/17/2020

authorHOUSE®

Dedication:

To my parents,
who made sure that I was "ready".
To my boys, who allowed me the
privilege to help them get "ready".
And to my husband, who knew that I
was "ready" all along!
I love you!

Betty gets ready
to school she goes,
she wants to get ready
from her head to her toes.

where the colors all match
and the buttons aren't gone.

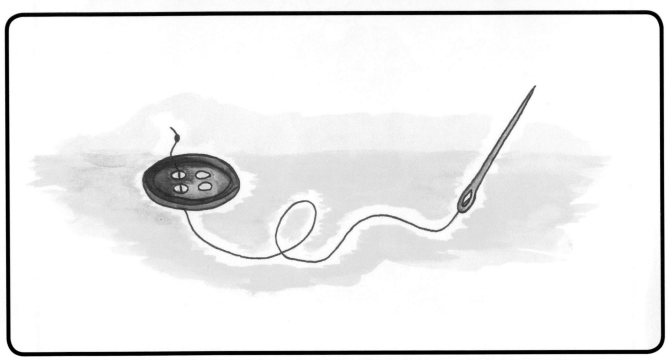

"Do stripes go with dots?
Does green go with blue?"

"I can't find my socks!
Oh where's my left shoe?"

When Betty gets ready,
she must do her hair,
but how should she do it?
What hair should she wear?

Maybe up--how about down?
Maybe curls...how about straight?
She must decide soon
so she doesn't run late!

As Betty gets ready
for her first day of school,
she makes sure to follow
that one special rule.

She must eat a good breakfast
to fill up her tummy.
She must make sure it's healthy
and make sure it's YUMMY.

"What shall I eat?"
Betty says with a sigh.

"There are pancakes, or muffins,
or eggs I can fry."

"Or maybe some oatmeal, that's always quite tasty, unless it gets bumpy, or lumpy, or pasty!"

When Betty gets ready
she must not forget,
to fill up her back pack
and get it all set.

"But what shall I bring
to school my first day?

I may need some markers, some
crayons, or some clay."

"I can't forget pencils, and paper, and glue...

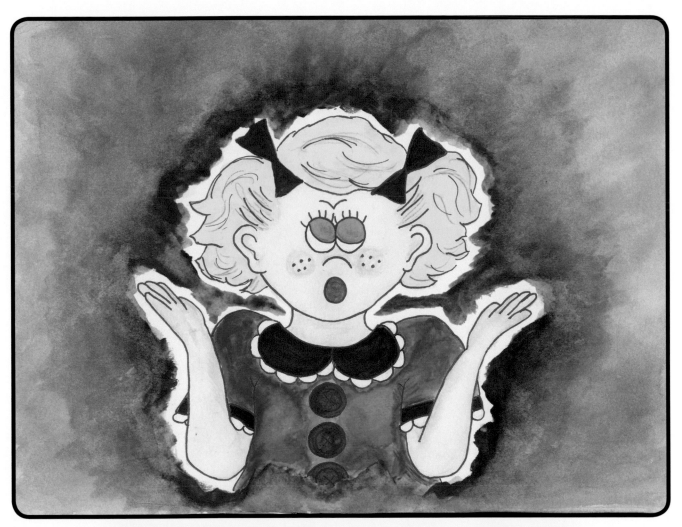

and what about gym class?
Oh where's my left shoe?"

"I can't wait for school!
It's so exciting you know...

but there's more to get ready
before I'm ready to go!"

So as Betty gets ready
she picks an apple so sweet,
to give to her teacher
that she's going to meet.

"I know she'll be kind
and help me learn something new,
she'll be smart, make me laugh,
and give me fun things to do."

Now as Betty gets ready
she goes to the shelf,
to get down her lunch box
and make her lunch by herself.

A sandwich, a pear,
maybe a cookie or two,
then miss Betty starts to giggle,
"oh there's my left shoe!"

The clock says it's time
for Betty to go,
"Are you ready, miss Betty?"
her mom says with a glow.

As Betty gets ready
to walk out the door,
she has thought of most everything-
but wait...there's one more!

Miss Betty turns around
to see her MOM and her dad.

They look so excited,
so proud and so glad...

Because Betty *is* ready
for school--can't you see?
When Betty gets ready,
she's as ready as can be!